The Proper Way to Slaughter Animal in Islam

Table of contents

CHAPTER ONE

The Correct Method of Slaughtering Animals in Islam

NTRODUCTION

Islam teaches us the process of slaughtering animals in the most e way possible.

The Islamic method of slaughtering animals has been a point of great criticism for many people, which has only been festering in this day and age where anima rights movements and scientific advancement are on the rise. Hence, this brings us to the question, what is Islam's take on the subject? Can we back it up with science?

According to Islamic law, the Arabic word for the ritual of slaughtering animals is known as Dhabihah, which essentially deems the slaughtered meat as 'halal' or permissible to eat. It is applicable on the slaughter of lawful (halal) animals like chicken, sheep, goat, cow etc., and becomes null and void on the slaughter of unlawful animals like pigs, dogs, cats etc. The method of zabihah is governed by a set of strict rules which need to be followed.

1. The slaughter needs to be carried out by a Muslim or Ahlul Kitab

Only a Muslim or someone who is Ahlul Kitab (people of the Book), can carry out the task for the meat to be deemed halal.

2. Start by reciting Allah's (SWT) name

The first step is to recite the name of Allah (SWT). This is to take Allah's (SWT) permission and to carry out the slaughter under His name and His name only; the slaughter cannot be made under the name of any other deity.

3. Slaughter the animal with a sharp knife (sharp cutting tool)

The animal must be sacrificed with a sharp knife in order to minimize the pain and it must be done quickly. A blunt knife will only prolong the whole ordeal, causing more pain to the animal.

4. Directly pierce the throat, windpipe and blood vessels of the animal

The person must place the knife directly over the throat and windpipe of the animal and make the cut precisely as possible, cutting off all the blood vessels but not the spinal cord itself (cutting the spinal cord can damage the nerve fibers which can cause the animal to go into cardiac arrest, stagnating the blood). This causes the animal to die quickly and with minimal pain.

5. Drain the blood

All the blood needs to be drained from the body before the head of the animal is removed. This is to purify the animal's body of any type of bacteria, toxins or germs that may reside in the blood of the animal, which can lead to different types of illnesses.

According to scientific evidence, the zabihah method of slaughter is actually one of the most e types of slaughter. The swift piercing of the windpipe and blood vessels cuts off the main source of blood, oxygen, and glucose which is necessary for the animal to stay alive, hence the animal instantly loses consciousness and cannot feel any pain after it. The movement and convulsions that follow are just muscular spasms due to the rapid flow of blood outside the body - it is not due to the pain.

Islam is a perfect religion. Allah (SWT) has ordained certain things to go a certain way because of reasons the brain cannot even fathom. The Dhabihah method of slaughter is perhaps the most e and merciful way of slaughtering animals, minimizing the pain and suffering of the living animal as much as possible. Only Allah (SWT), the Creator, the Wisest, could have deemed it to be so.

Islamic Method of Slaughtering

Islamic law requires that animals intended for consumption be slain in a certain manner. Halal slaughter is being one of the more e methods available to the meat industry and the only method acceptable for Muslim consumers. The conditions for Halal slaughter can be summarized as follows:

The animal to be slaughtered must be from the categories that are permitted for Muslims to eat.

The animal must be alive at the time of slaughter.

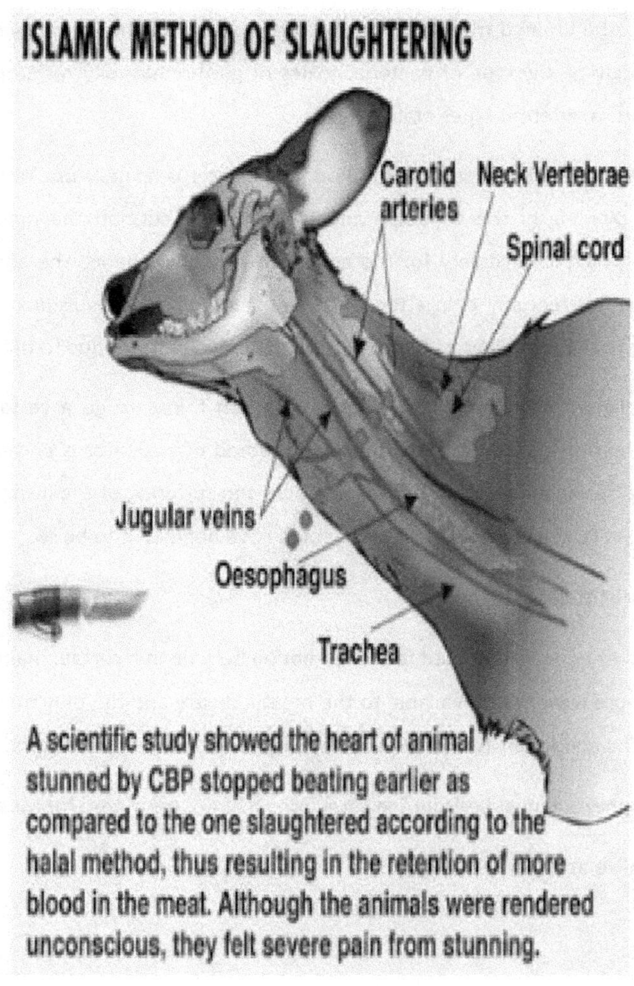
ISLAMIC METHOD OF SLAUGHTERING
Carotid arteries
Neck Vertebrae
Spinal cord
Jugular veins
Oesophagus
Trachea
A scientific study showed the heart of animal
stunned by CBP stopped beating earlier as
compared to the one slaughtered according to the
halal method, thus resulting in the retention of more
blood in the meat. Although the animals were rendered
unconscious, they felt severe pain from stunning.

<u>**The Proper Way to Slaughter Animal in Islam**</u>

In general, all forms of stunning and unconsciousness of animals are disliked. However, if it is necessary to use these means to calm down or mitigate violence of animals, low voltage shock can be used on the head only for the duration and voltage as per given guidelines. Stunning through a device with a non-penetrating round head, in a way that does not kill the animal before its slaughter, is permitted, provided that certain conditions are adhered to. Please refer to DHCE Halal Standards for more details.

The animal must be slaughtered by the use of a sharp knife. The knife must not kill due to its weight. If it kills due to the impact the meat may not be permissible.

The windpipe (throat), food-tract (oesophagus) and the two jugular veins must be cut.

The slaughtering must be done in one stroke without lifting the knife. The knife should not be placed and lifted when slaughtering the animal.

Slaughtering must be done by a sane adult Muslim. Animals slaughtered by a Non-Muslim will not be Halal.

The name of Allah must be invoked (mentioned) at the time of slaughtering by saying: Bismillah Allahu Akbar. (In the Name of Allah; Allah is the Greatest.)

If at the time of slaughtering the name of anyone else other than Allah is invoked (i.e. animal sacrificed for him/her), then the meat becomes Haram "unlawful."

If a Muslim forgets to invoke the name of Allah at the time of slaughtering, the meat will remain Halal. However, if he intentionally does not invoke the name of Allah, the meat becomes Haram.

The head of the animal must not be cut off during slaughtering but later after the animal is completely dead, even the knife should not go deep into the spinal cord.

Skinning or cutting any part of the animal is not allowed before the animal is completely dead.

Slaughtering must be made in the neck from the front (chest) to the back.

The slaughtering must be done manually not by a machine, as one of the conditions is the intention, which is not found in a machine.

The slaughtering should not be done on a production line where pigs are slaughtered. Any instrument used for slaughtering pigs should not be used in the Halal slaughtering.

Customary and Desirable Practices When Slaughtering

- Water should be offered to the animal before slaughter, and it should not be slaughtered when hungry.
- The knife should be hidden from the animal, and slaughtering should be done out of sight of other animals waiting to be slaughtered.
- Animals should be killed in a comfortable way. Unnecessary suffering to them must be avoided.
- The animal must be slaughtered by the use of a sharp knife. The knife must not kill due to its weight. If it kills due to the impact the meat may not be permissible.
- The knife should be re-sharpened before slaughter.
- Meat chilled or frozen for export to Muslims should be stored in separate cold stores other than those in which pork or other non-Halal meat is stored.
- Meat minced or processed for Muslims should not be minced in the same machines used to mince pork or other non-Halal meat.

CHAPTER TWO

The Muslim slaughter

ismillahi (In the name of Allah)

(مُؤْمِنِينَ بِآيَاتِهِ كُنتُم إِن عَلَيْهِ اللّهِ اسْمُ ذُكِرَ مِمّا فَكُلُوا)

(So eat of that [meat] upon which the name of Allah has been mentioned, if you are believers in His verses)

(6 -118) the Cattle – al-An'Am – الأنعام

(In the name of Allah, Allah is the Greatest)

Dhabīḥah (or zabiha, Arabic: ذَحِيْبَة) is, in Islamic law, the prescribed method of ritual slaughter of all lawful halal animals (goats, sheep, cows, chicken) excluding locusts, fish, and most sea-life. Unlawful animals like pigs, dog, kangaroo, boar, etc. are not allowed to be slaughtered or zabihah. This method of slaughtering lawful animals has several conditions to be fulfilled. The butcher must be Muslim, the name of God or "In the name of God" (Bismillah) must be called by the butcher upon slaughter of each halal animal separately, and it should consist of a swift, deep incision with a very sharp knife on the throat, cutting the wind pipe, jugular veins and carotid arteries of both sides but leaving the spinal cord intact.

According to the Islamic law, halal ritual slaughter is an act of adoration. It is performed manually.

It is to be performed for Allah (Subhanahu wa Ta'ala), the One and Only God, only for Him and in a manner that He approved and allowed, and with the intention of ensuring proper nutrition.

Offertory is the worship of the One and Only God, therefore it cannot be replaced by a machine with a sharp mechanical knife. Ritual slaughter must be performed properly. In order to kill small animals (sheep, poultry and cattle), the neck should be cut below the larynx: pharynx, oesophagus and large blood vessels, with one move. The larynx must stay close to the head.

Ritual slaughter is perfect if it meets the following conditions:

The Proper Way to Slaughter Animal in Islam

1. Ritual slaughterer:

– A ritual slaughterer should be a practising Muslim, a mature and sensible man, competent in the area of ritual slaughter.

– A ritual slaughterer must pray five (5) times a day, in a timely manner.

– Mature: an immature person should not perform ritual slaughter.

– Sensible: killing an animal by a madman, drunkard, drug addict, child (immature) or a mentally ill person is against the law.

– Specialist: he must be approved and authorized to perform ritual slaughter.

– A ritual slaughterer must demonstrate perfect hygiene and wear appropriate clothing. He should be dressed in accordance with health protection regulations.

2. Ritual slaughter tools and devices:

– An animal must be trapped in an appropriate trap device.

– A box or a cage must be easy to use and open without noise to prevent stress of the animal.

– In order to avoid stress, pain and wing fracture, birds can also be trapped in an appropriate device. Poultry can be hanged by the legs on a slaughter line.

– Knives used for slaughter must be sharp, have rigid blades and be resistant to corrosion, so as to ensure quick and immediate death of an animal. They cannot be used for any other purposes than ritual slaughter.

– Knives must be sharpened before every slaughter to prevent pain.

– The room where slaughter takes place must be equipped with a sufficient number of knives and sharpening machines.

3. Animals

– All animals intended for slaughter must undergo examination (ante mortem) performed by veterinary services.

– Ill animals, in the state of clinical death, bitten by a wild animal, afflicted by diseases contagious for people (zoonosis) and with high temperature are not killed, because they are not halal, i.e. not healthy.

– Tired and stressed animals after the transport must rest before the slaughter.

– In order to avoid visual stress in animals before ritual slaughter, one should avoid situations in which animals could see a knife or a death of other animals.

– Land animals, accepted for consumption, killed by: suffocation, stunning by hitting in the head, electric shock, immersion in hot water or gassing that is not allowed (Arab. haram) are not accepted for consumption.

– Brutal treatment of these animals is unacceptable. Proper treatment of animals is the chief rule.

4. conditions during ritual slaughter of cattle:

Cattle slaughterhouses in Poland are equipped with a holding system used to immobilize an animal before ritual slaughter.

a) Hygiene before ritual slaughter

Ritual slaughterers must take care of personal hygiene and wear appropriate clothing that meets sanitary regulations. Food hygiene in Islam is based on the fact that animals bleed quickly, without stunning and stress, and the meat remains clean. Blood is a habitat of diseases and a threat to health.

b) The conditions of animal slaughter legal validity according to the Islamic law:

An animal must be kept in a trap appropriate for a given species. It is recommended that a ritual slaughterer directs an animal towards quibla (the direction of Mecca). A ritual slaughterer must be in the state of cleanliness (tahir: ghusl). He should preferably perform ablution (wudhu). A ritual slaughterer, in order to express his intention to sacrifice, must pronounce the name of God and say: "Bismillah, Allah Akbar" (In the name of Allah, Allah is the Greatest). If this is forgotten unintentionally – it does not have any consequences. If this is omitted intentionally – the meat is not accepted for consumption (it is treated as non-halal).

Killing animals in Islam is a method of ritual slaughter of edible land animals, practised by means of a deep and quick incision of throat with a sharp knife, in order to cut the carotid quickly and to leave the spinal cord. The purpose of this technique is to easily remove blood from an animal's body in a way to leave the meat clean.

Animals are killed with one or two moves with a sharp knife (there and back). A tool used for slaughter must be sharp to prevent additional pain and long suffering. The cut should not be made in the presence of another animal, as the sight of slaughter evokes unnecessary stress and anxiety. A knife should not be sharpened in front of an animal.

Animals are killed through the simultaneous cut of the trachea under the larynx and on both sides of carotid arteries and jugular veins. One should wait several minutes after the slaughter to allow the leakage of blood from the cut carotid. The animal stays in the trap until it loses blood to death. After it stops fighting, it falls on the floor and is immediately hanged to lose all the blood. The suffering experienced by an animal is limited to the knife going through the skin. Contractions of limbs after slaughter and bleeding do not signify pain. It is a natural nervous reflex due to the lack of blood supply and brain oxygenation. These contractions help to expel the maximum amount of blood from the body.

It is not allowed to make any cuts on an animal (e.g. cutting legs or head) before its complete death (the last gleam of the retina is the sign of death).

If carotid arteries are blocked (a physiological reaction of the narrowing of vessels), the ritual slaughterer makes an incision in the neck tip in order to release blood. One cannot start the process of cutting up or break the spine before the complete descent of its soul.

c) Hygiene after ritual slaughter

Once the skin is removed, gutting should be made immediately and quickly in order to prevent intestinal bacteria from penetrating into deep tissues. Meat in containers should not have a direct contact with the ground. Staff responsible for supervision and sanitary inspection is obliged to carry out regular general hygiene inspections and microbiological inspections of halal products and used devices, i.e. the "contact points". The facility must inform about the planned inspection, its nature, frequency and the results of microbiological controls.

CHAPTER THREE

Summary of conditions for halal slaughter

slamic law requires that animals intended for consumption be slain in a certain manner.

The conditions for halal slaughter can be summarized as follows:

1. The animal to be slaughtered must be from the categories that are permitted for Muslims to eat.

2. The animal must be alive at the time of slaughter.

3. No electric shock, bullet or any other means should be used before slaughtering. Using any such method may lead to the death of the animal before it is cut. Islam prohibits Muslims from eating any meat coming   from an animal that is dead before slaughter. Muslims are also advised to avoid eating anything doubtful.

4. The animal must be slaughtered by the use of a sharp knife. The knife must not kill due to its weight. If it kills due to the impact the meat may not be permissible.

5. The windpipe (throat), food-tract (esophagus) and the two jugular veins must be cut.

6. The slaughtering must be done in one stroke without lifting the knife. The knife should not be placed and lifted when slaughtering the animal.

7. Slaughtering must be done by a sane adult Muslim. Animals slaughtered by a Non-Muslim will not be halal.

8. The name of Allah must be invoked (mentioned) at the time of slaughtering by saying: "Bismillah Allahu Akbar". (In the Name of Allah; Allah is the Greatest.)

9. If at the time of slaughtering the name of anyone else other than Allah is invoked (i.e. animal sacrificed for him/her), then the meat becomes haram "unlawful."

10. If a Muslim forgets to invoke the name of Allah at the time of slaughtering, the meat will remain halal.   However, if he intentionally does not invoke the name of Allah, the meat becomes haram.

11. The head of the animal must not be cut off during slaughtering but later after the animal is completely dead, even the knife should not go deep into the spinal cord.
12. Skinning or cutting any part of the animal is not allowed before the animal is completely dead.
13. Slaughtering must be made in the neck from the front (chest) to the back.
14. The slaughtering must be done manually not by a machine, as one of the conditions is the intention, which is not found in a machine.
15. The slaughtering should not be done on a production line where pigs are slaughtered. Any instrument used for slaughtering pigs should not be used in the halal slaughtering.

16. Customary and desirable practices when slaughtering
17. Water should be offered to the animal before slaughter, and it should not be slaughtered when hungry.
18. The knife should be hidden from the animal, and slaughtering should be done out of sight of other animals waiting to be slaughtered.

19. Animals should be killed in a comfortable way. Unnecessary suffering to them must be avoided.
20. The knife should be re-sharpened before slaughter.

Storage, processing and transport of halal meat

1.– Meat chilled or frozen for export to Muslims should be stored in separate cold stores other than those in which pork or other non-halal meat is stored.

2.– Meat minced or processed for Muslims should not be minced in the same machines used to mince pork   or other non-halal meat.

What exactly does the halal method of animal slaughter involve?

Contrary to what many assume, an estimated 88% of animals killed by halal methods in Britain are stunned before slaughter

James Meikle (May 2014).

The Proper Way to Slaughter Animal in Islam

The debate over when meat is halal and whether it should be clearly labelled has been put back on the agenda by vets and animal welfare campaigners who want all animals slaughtered for food to be stunned before killing.

The Arabic word halal means permissible, and the rules of slaughter are based on Islamic law. The animal has to be alive and healthy, a Muslim has to perform the slaughter in the appropriate ritual manner, and the animal's throat must be cut by a sharp knife severing the carotid artery, jugular vein and windpipe in a single swipe. Blood must be drained out of the carcass.

About 40m cattle, sheep, and calves and 900m poultry birds are killed in British abattoirs each year, according to a Food Standards Agency (FSA) report two years ago, and one estimate has suggested that 114m of these animals, including poultry, are killed using the halal method. The value of the market could be £2bn a year or more.

But contrary to what many assume, most animals killed by halal methods are stunned before slaughter. FSA estimates suggest that 88% of animals in the UK killed by halal methods were stunned beforehand in a way that many Muslims find religiously acceptable.

In many sheep and lambs this is by electronic stunning to the head or in poultry via a water bath electrified with enough power to make them unconscious but not to kill. Another method of stunning that involves cardiac arrest is not allowed under halal rules.

In non-halal slaughterhouses, stunned animals are shackled and hoisted above the ground where a slaughter man "sticks" them, cutting their throat or inserting a chest stick close to the heart. Cattle and some sheep and pigs are stunned by a bolt through the brain before being killed.

Many poultry are now killed using gas. But they have traditionally been shackled, hung upside down on a production line, moved through electrified water to stun them, then conveyed to a mechanical neck cutter. In halal, however, they are killed by hand.

Muslims who oppose any stunning say their method remains the most e and point out that a number of stunning methods have been banned as being bad for animal welfare.

The Jewish method of slaughter called shechita cannot involve pre-slaughter stunning at all. Its proponents say the technique learned by practitioners over seven years of training meets the European Union's requirement for stunning in that it brings insensitivity to pain and distress. They argue that a surgically sharp instrument, twice the width of the animal's neck and known as the chalaf, is sufficient because of the speed and expertise with which is applied.

It is estimated that in total, under any method, 3% of cattle, 10% of sheep and goats and 4% of poultry slaughtered in Britain are not pre-stunned, although a proportion are stunned after the cut.

Vets say untanned cattle take about 20 seconds (but up to 2 minutes) to lose consciousness, sheep six or seven seconds (but up to 20) and poultry seven or eight seconds, but all these times can be far longer.

Some European countries, most recently Denmark, have banned slaughter without pre-stunning. The RSPCA and British Veterinary Association are among the groups calling for an end to slaughter without pre-stunning — a move that would mean an end to religious exemptions from European and UK legislation on this element of slaughtering, and also, say campaigners, an end to unnecessary suffering.

Campaigners are urging the government to introduce clear labelling to say whether meat is slaughtered by halal methods — an issue which the European Union is already studying. Some Muslims warn that there must be an information campaign beforehand and those who are against any stunning question why, if labelling on the halal method is necessary, why is not for animals slaughtered in other ways, by captive-bolt gun, gassing, electrocution, drowning or "sim-stunning".

CHAPTER FOUR

Conditions for proper slaughter

Different conditions apply to the slaughterer, the animal being slaughtered and the tool used for slaughter.

Conditions applicable to the slaughterer

1- The slaughterer, whether man or woman, Muslim or a follower of another divine religion, must be a sane person of sound judgement. Regarding Muslims, God says after mentioning the animals that are forbidden to eat:

'except that which you may have slaughtered when it is still alive'

(Qur'an 5:3)

In respect of non-Muslims,

: Allah (SWT) says,

'The food of those who were given the Scriptures before you is lawful to you'

(Qur'an5:5)

Ibn Abbas said: 'The food to which the verse refers is their slaughtered animals.' It is not permissible to eat of the animals slaughtered by other unbelievers, or by a mad or drunk person, or by a child.

2-The slaughterer must not dedicate his slaughtered animal to anyone other than Allah, or in the name of anyone else. If the slaughterer dedicates it to an idol, or a Muslim or non-Muslim person, or to a Prophet (peace be upon him) it becomes forbidden to eat. In giving the details of what is forbidden,

: Allah includes the animal

'and that which has been dedicated to other than Allah.'

(Qur'an 16:115)

When these two conditions are met, the slaughtered animal is lawful to eat, and it does not matter if the slaughterer is a man, a woman, old, young, or free.

Two: Conditions applicable to the slaughtered animal

1.To cut the animal's throat, oesophagus, trachea, and the two jugular veins.

Rafi' ibn Khadij reports that the Prophet (peace be upon him) said

'When the animal's blood has been profusely shed and Allah's name is mentioned at the time of slaughter, then eat of it, but do not use teeth and claws.'

Related by al-Bukhari, hadith No. 2,488; Muslim, hadith No. 1,968

2. Allah's name must be mentioned when the slaughter is about to be made.

Allah says,

'And do not eat of that upon which the name of Allah has not been mentioned, for indeed, it is grave disobedience.'

(Qur'an 6: 121).

It is recommended also to glorify Allah, saying Allah-u akbar, as the Prophet (peace be upon him) is reported to have done so.

Related by al-Bukhari, hadith No. 5,565; Muslim, hadith No. 1,966.

Three: The condition applicable to the tool

The Proper Way to Slaughter Animal in Islam

When slaughtering an animal, a blade of iron or brass or sharp stone should be used, provided that it is sharp enough to cut the throat and the jugular veins swiftly to let the blood pour out. It should not be a blade made of a bone like an animal's teeth, or of claws like those of birds.

Things to avoid

1.It is reprehensible to slaughter the animal with a blunt blade, because this tortures the animal.

Ibn Umar reports: 'Allah's messenger commanded that blades should be sharpened and kept unseen by the animals.'

Related by Ahmad, hadith No. 5,864; Ibn Majah, hadith No. 3,172.

2. It is also reprehensible to break the animal's neck or to start to skin it before it is dead. Shaddad ibn Aws quotes the Prophet (peace be upon him) as saying:

'When you slaughter, slaughter well.'

 Related by (Muslim)

Umar said: 'Do not be hasty before the slaughtered animal has died.'

Related by al-Bayhaqi in Al-Sunan al-Kubra, vol. 9, p. 278.

3. The slaughterer should not sharpen his blade with the animal looking at what he is doing.Slaughter by followers of other religions nor slaughter an animal while the other animal is watching.

Slaughter by followers of other religions

The animals slaughtered by Jews and Christians are lawful for Muslims to eat, as Allah says:

'The food of those who were given the Scriptures before you is lawful to you.'

(Qur'an 5:5)

Except in cases where they slaughter in the name of what they celebrate for during their festival.

Cruelty to animals occurs during production, handling, transport, and slaughter in most countries where Islam is a major religion. Most of the people involved in this, such as those involved in the transport of animals, animal handlers, and butchers, are Muslims. However, many Muslims and Islamic religious leaders are not aware of this cruelty. Islam is a religion that shows compassion to animals as mentioned in the holy book Qur'an and sayings of the Prophet Mohammed (pbuh). This paper highlights what Islam says of the welfare of animals and how animal welfare can be improved by sensitizing all Muslims and religious leaders to the teachings on animal welfare in the Qur'an and the Hadiths so that they can influence their followers.

Islam is a comprehensive religion guiding the lives of its followers through sets of rules governing the personal, social, and public aspects through the verses of the Holy Qur'an and Hadiths, the compilation of the traditions of Prophet Muhammad (Peace Be Upon Him), the two main documents that serve as guidelines. Islam is explicit with regard to using animals for purposes and there is a rich tradition of the Prophet Mohammad's (Peace Be Upon Him) concern for animals to be found in the Hadith and Sunna. Islam has also laid down rules for e slaughter. In many countries animals are killed without pre-stunning. Regardless of pre-stunning, such meat should not be treated as halāl or at least be considered as Makrooh (detestable or abominable), because the animals have been beaten or treated without compassion during production, handling, transport, and slaughter. Many Muslims and Islamic religious leaders are not aware of the cruelty that is routinely inflicted on animals during transport, pre-slaughter, and slaughter in many Islamic countries. There is an urgent need to sensitize all Muslims to the teachings of animal welfare in the Qur'an and the Hadiths. A campaign is needed to apprise religious leaders of the current cruelty that occurs during transport and slaughter.

There is considerable debate on the role of religion in animal welfare, with implications for the study of welfare for welfare assessment and for implementation of solutions to welfare problems. In Islam, the law is a privileged means of access to the sacred. For most Muslims, Islamic normativity (fiqh or shari'a) is an essential part of being a Muslim. The demand for and production of authoritative rulings is one form of social expression of normative Islam.

1. There are many published papers on how Islam provides an ethic of environmental concern and non-animal protection. Islamic law is most prescriptive in its insistence on e treatment. The killing of non-animals for meat and hides by halāl (that is, permissible based on a set of ethical and religious standards) methods is obligatory, with meat considered forbidden (Makrooh) if the non-animal has in any way been subjected to in treatment [3]. Regenstein [16] cites several sources that stipulate the need to ensure e and efficient practices are fulfilled, including edicts from the second and fourth Caliphs. Generally, the killing of wildlife for any other reasons than food is always prohibited, as is the caging of birds, sports hunting, and animal baiting

2. The Relevance of Animal Welfare under Islam

<u>**The Proper Way to Slaughter Animal in Islam**</u>

Islam provides considerable support for the importance of animal welfare. There is a rich tradition of the Prophet Mohammad's (Peace Be Upon Him) concern for animals to be found in the Hadith and Sunna, and Islam provides considerable support for the importance of animal welfare.

The Qur'an [14] is explicit with regard to using animals for purposes. A closer look at the teachings of the Qur'an and tradition reveals teachings of kindness and concern for animals.

For example:

'And cattle He has created for you (men); from them ye derive warmth and numerous benefits, and of their (meat) ye eat.' (Surrah An-Nahl 16:5)

'And they carry your heavy loads to lands that ye could not (otherwise) reach except with souls distressed: for your Lord is indeed Most Kind, Most Merciful.' (Surrah An-Nahl 16:7)

'And (He has created) horses, mules, and donkeys, for you to ride and as an adornment; And he has created other things of which ye have no knowledge.' (Surrah An-Nahl 16:8)

'We have made animals subject to you, that ye may be grateful.' (Surrah Al

Haj 22:36)

'There is not a moving (living) creature on earth, nor a bird that flies with its two wings, but are communities like you. We have neglected nothing in the Book, then unto their Lord they (all) shall be gathered.' (Surrah Al-Anam 6:38)

'Seest thou not that it is Allah Whose praise all beings in the heavens and on earth do celebrate, and the birds (of the air) with wings outspread? Each one knows its own (mode of) prayer and praise, and Allah knows well all that they do.' (Surrah An-Noor 24:41)

Qur'an actually forbids actions which may lead to harm; 'transgress not in the balance, and weigh with justice, and skimp not in the balance … earth, He set it down for all beings' (Surrah Ar-Rahman 55:8–10)

We now have a view of animals that shows them not merely as resources, but as creatures dependent on God (Allah). Animals are seen to have their own lives and purpose, valuable to themselves and to Allah above and beyond any material value they may provide to it.

The Qur'an is not the only Islamic source for messages of kindness towards animals.

<u>**The Proper Way to Slaughter Animal in Islam**</u>

There is a rich tradition of the Prophet Mohammed's (Peace Be Upon Him) concern for animals to be found in the Hadith and Sunna. For example,

The Prophet Muhammad (Peace Be Upon Him) condemned the beating of animals and forbade striking, branding, or marking them on the face.

He cursed and chastised those who mistreated animals and gave praise to those who showed kindness;

He also instituted radical changes against the practice of cutting off the tails and humps of living animals for food.

One Hadith Quotes Prophet Muhammad (Peace Be Upon Him) as saying:

"A good deed done to an animal is as meritorious as a good deed done to a being, while an act of cruelty to an animal is as bad as an act of cruelty to a being."

Prophet Muhammad (Peace be upon him) was especially vocal in his disapproval of the cruel practices of notching and slitting of ears of animals and the practice of putting painful rings around the necks of camels. (Hadith: Bukhari)

Below are just a few well-known examples from the hadith (traditions):

 "There is a reward (ajr) for helping any living creature." (Hadith: Bukhari and Muslim)

"It is a great sin for man to imprison those animals which are in his power." (Hadith: Muslim)

"The worst of shepherds is the ungentle, who causes the beasts to crush or bruise one another." (Hadith: Muslim)

"You will not have secure faith until you love one another and have mercy on those who live upon the earth." (Hadiths: Bukhari, Muslim, and Abu Dawud)

"Fear God in these mute animals, and ride them when they are fit to be ridden, and let them go free when … they (need to) rest." (Hadith: Abu Dawud)

"There is no man who kills a sparrow or anything beyond that, without its deserving it, but God will ask him about it." (Hadiths: Ahmad and al-Nasai)

The grievous things are: shirk (polytheism); disobedience to parents; the killing of breathing beings …" (Hadiths: Bukhari and Muslim)

"May Allah curse anyone who maims animals." (Hadith: Bukhari)

"Whoever is kind to the creatures of God is kind to himself." (Hadith: Bukhari)

"There is none amongst the Muslims, who plants a tree or sow's seeds, and then a bird, or a person or an animal eats from it, but is regarded as a charitable gift for him" (Hadith: Bukhari)

These examples clearly indicate how Islam treats any animal with kindness.

3. Islam and Rules Concerning the Slaughter of Animals

The e slaughter of animals is strongly supported in the Islamic tradition. For example, Sahih Muslim (Book 21, Chapter 11, Number 4810) records Prophet Mohammad (Peace Be Upon) saying:

"Verily Allah has enjoined goodness to everything; so when you kill, kill in a good way and when you slaughter, slaughter in a good way. So every one of you should sharpen his knife, and let the slaughtered animal die comfortably."

Prophet Muhammad (Peace be Upon Him) has also said, "When one of you slaughters, let him complete it", meaning that one should sharpen the knife well and feed, water, and soothe the animal before killing it.

He also said, "Do you intend (on) inflicting death on the animal twice—once by sharpening the knife within its sight, and once by cutting its throat?"

Islam has also laid down Other Rules for e slaughter as indicated by a combination of Hadiths, including the following:

Animals should have a pre-slaughter rest, and be well fed and well looked after at the point of slaughter.

The animals must be alive or deemed to be alive at the time of slaughter.

Slaughter must be performed by a Muslim (who is of sound mind, mature, and fully understands the Islamic procedure and conditions for slaughtering of animals).

that are slaughtered should be securely restrained, particularly the head and neck, before cutting the throat.

Operator competence is of great importance in order to carry out satisfactory halāl slaughter.

tools and other implements used must be for the slaughter of halāl animals only.

The knife must be razor sharp and without blemishes and damage. For animals with normal necks, the act of slaughter must begin with an incision on the animal's neck just before the glottis, and for animals with long necks such as chicken, turkeys, ostriches, camels, etc., the inc sion must be before the glottis.

The animal's trachea and esophagus must be severed. The spinal corc should not be cut and the head not severed completely so as to induce immediate and massive hemorrhage. In certain mazhab (school of thought), uttering the phrase "bismillah" immediately before the slaughter is compulsory. In others, such utterance is highly encouraged.

must be done once only. The slaughtering implement must not be lifted off the animal during slaughtering. Any lifting is construed as one act of slaughter. Multiple acts of slaughter on one animal are prohibited.

Slaughter the animal in such a way that its life departs quickly, and it is not left to suffer.

must be spontaneous and complete.

should not be shackled and hoisted before bleeding.

should be done only after the animal has lost consciousness. Restraining equipment should be comfortable for the animal.

Further preparation and dressing of the carcass must be delayed until all signs of life and cerebral reflex have disappeared.

Shackling and hoisting conscious animals seems to violate both the e intent of Islamic slaughter law, and Prophet Muhammad's (pbuh) comments on the process of slaughter.

Regarding stunning, Al-Masri [3] notes that stunning has been declared as acceptable by a fatwa (unanimous verdict) of the Al-Azhar University in Cairo. Furthermore, the Muslim World League declared in 1986 that pre-slaughter stunning is lawful when the weakest electric current renders a non-animal unconscious before slaughter [3]. Requirements and methods of stunning which are acceptable by Islamic authorities in countries such as Malaysia have been published [17].

The Proper Way to Slaughter Animal in Islam

Eating meat produced using cruel methods violates the Prophet Muhammad's (pbuh) general precept to cause animals no pain before their slaughter, as well as more specific injunctions regarding the treatment of food animals. Indeed, if animals have been subjected to cruelty in transport and slaughter, or to general cruelty, meat from them is considered by Islam as impure and unlawful to eat (Makrooh). The flesh of animals killed by cruel methods (Al-Muthiah) is carrion (Al-Mujaththamah). Even if these animals have been slaughtered in the strictest Islamic manner, if cruelties were otherwise inflicted on them, their flesh is still forbidden (Haram) food.

"Oh, ye messengers! Eat of the good things {tayyibat} and do righteous deeds. Surely, I know what you do" (Qur'an 23:51).

"Oh believers! Eat what We have provided for you of lawful and good things, and give thanks for Allah's favour, if it is He whom you serve" (Qur'an 2:172; 16:114).

The word "Tayyib", translated as "good", "pure", or "wholesome", means "pure", both in the physical and the moral sense.

In summary, the main counsel of Islam for the slaughter of animals for food is to do it in the least painful manner. All the Islamic laws on the treatment of animals, including the method of slaughter, are based on compassion, fellow-feeling, and benevolence.

Go to:

4. What is Prevalent Today?

Many current practices are not in accordance with the above teachings and may result in great cruelty to animals. Handling of animals before and during transport is often cruel. Some animals are marched on foot for several days. During such transport, animals may lose weight and may be beaten unnecessarily. Many animals are not fed and watered en route. Animals—young and old, big or small—may be tied in twos and fours in order to reduce the number of animal minders or personnel on the trail. Such tying results in injury and fatigue to the animals. Some animals are beaten and forced to move quickly in order to reach markets and abattoirs on time. Those that fall down may be whipped to force them to rise [1].

Similarly, needless suffering is inflicted on animals that are transported three or four days together in overcrowded, ill-ventilated, trucks, especially in hot, humid weather.

Harsh conditions also occur at slaughter plants. Animals may be held in primitive facilities without shade, and animals may be restrained by short tethers. At the point of slaughter, animals are often struck and beaten to make them enter the slaughter facilities.

5. What Needs to be Done?

Many Muslims and Islamic religious leaders are not aware of the cruelty that is routinely inflicted on animals during transport, at pre-slaughter, and at slaughter in many Islamic countries. There is an urgent need to sensitise all Muslims to the teachings on animal welfare in the Qur'an and the Hadiths. This approach is bound to be effective in influencing the majority of Muslims in the livestock trade, especially the slaughter man in treating animals more ely. This needs to be done by intervention at the highest level by religious bodies and organisations, which could be most effective in giving rulings (fatwas) on this issue [1]. Poor practices and animal welfare abuses occurring during halāl meat production has been reviewed [18], with ways and means suggested to improve animal welfare especially using Mosque-based sermons by Imams to increase awareness of animal welfare issues. The Dialrel project [19] reviewed current practices during halāl and Sechita slaughter in cattle, sheep, goat, and poultry in Belgium, Germany, Italy, the Netherlands, Spain, UK, Turkey, and Australia, and the report discussed various stakeholders including Muslim and Jewish representatives.

CHAPTER FIVE

Measures to be taken to achieve Progress during Transport and Slaughter

A campaign is needed to apprise religious leaders of the current cruelty that occurs during transport and slaughter, for example by slides and videos. This should be done by competent and knowledgeable individuals who are also aware of the Islamic principles of animal welfare, preferably by Muslims in order to give authenticity to their claims.

The creation of animal welfare legislation, including animal transport and slaughter, according to the World Organisation for Animal Health (OIE) standards and Islamic principles.

Government officials in charge of livestock, especially at abattoirs, should be sensitized to the concepts of animal welfare and how these relate to Islamic principles.

Abattoirs should be equipped with the facilities required for the good application of animal welfare standards, including unloading facilities, slaughtering boxes, and well-trained personnel to implement correct halāl slaughter.

The OIE animal welfare standards, especially those dealing with land transport and slaughter of animals for consumption, which were adopted in 2005 by OIE Members, need to be more strictly implemented by governments.

The OIE encourages Veterinary Services to enter into dialogue with religious authorities with the objective of raising awareness of the importance of animal welfare and reducing animal suffering globally. In order to achieve this, the OIE would, if required, assist member countries by providing expertise of Muslims knowledgeable both in Islamic Shariah and Animal Welfare.

6. Conclusions

Since cruelty to animals occurs during production, handling, transport, and slaughter in most countries where Islam is a major religion, Muslims and Islamic religious leaders need to be sensitized to this issue with reference to the teachings of animal welfare in the Qur'an and the Hadiths. To achieve this objective a campaign is needed with the help of animal welfare organizations and the World Organization for Animal Health (OIE). This will greatly influence the majority of Muslims in the livestock trade in treating animals more ely.

Keywords

Some keywords in Arabic used in the book and their Meanings

Makrooh- Prohibited

Bismillahi- In the name of Allah

Halal - lawful

Haram - unlawful

Zabihah -

Dhabihah - Ritual way of Slaughtering

Ajar - Reward

Shirk - Polytheism

Al Muthiah - Animals killed by the method of cruelty

Tayyib - Good, Pure or wholesome

Tayyibat - Eat of the good things

Fatawah - Islamic ruling

Shechita - Jews method of Slaughter

Ahalul kittab - People of the book

References

The correct method of Slaughtering Animal in Islam: Amna Anwar

Rules for Slaughtering Animals in Islam: Islamic journals.

www.ingramcontent.com/pod-product-compliance
Lightning Source LLC
Chambersburg PA
CBHW072346270726
48659CB00023B/2406